AWESOME ANIMAL HEROES

JANE
GOODALL

REBECCA FELIX

Consulting Editor, Diane Craig, M.A./Reading Specialist

Super Sandcastle

An Imprint of Abdo Publishing
abdopublishing.com

abdopublishing.com

Published by Abdo Publishing, a division of ABDO, PO Box 398166, Minneapolis, Minnesota 55439.
Copyright © 2017 by Abdo Consulting Group, Inc. International copyrights reserved in all countries.
No part of this book may be reproduced in any form without written permission from the publisher.
Super SandCastle™ is a trademark and logo of Abdo Publishing.

Printed in the United States of America, North Mankato, Minnesota
102016
012017

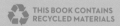
THIS BOOK CONTAINS
RECYCLED MATERIALS

Editor: Paige Polinsky
Content Developer: Nancy Tuminelly
Cover and Interior Design and Production: Mighty Media, Inc.
Photo Credits: AP Images, Everett Collection NYC, Jane Goodall Institute, Science Museum of Minnesota, Shutterstock

Publisher's Cataloging-in-Publication Data

Names: Felix, Rebecca, author.
Title: Jane Goodall / by Rebecca Felix.
Description: Minneapolis, MN : Abdo Publishing, 2017. | Series: Awesome animal
    heroes
Identifiers: LCCN 2016944697 | ISBN 9781680784336 (lib. bdg.) |
    ISBN 9781680797862 (ebook)
Subjects: LCSH: Goodall, Jane, 1934- --Juvenile literature. | Primatologists--
    England--Biography--Juvenile literature. | Women primatologists--England--
    Biography--Juvenile literature. | Chimpanzees--Tanzania--Gombe Stream
    National Park--Juvenile literature.
Classification: DDC 590.92 [B]--dc23
LC record available at http://lccn.loc.gov/2016944697

Super SandCastle™ books are created by a team of professional educators, reading specialists, and content developers around five essential components—phonemic awareness, phonics, vocabulary, text comprehension, and fluency—to assist young readers as they develop reading skills and strategies and increase their general knowledge. All books are written, reviewed, and leveled for guided reading, early reading intervention, and Accelerated Reader™ programs for use in shared, guided, and independent reading and writing activities to support a balanced approach to literacy instruction.

CONTENTS

CHIMP EXPERT

Jane Goodall is a **primatologist**. She has discovered more about **primates** than anyone in the world! Goodall lived among these animals in the wild for years. She works to teach people about protecting them and their **habitat**.

Jane Goodall

JANE GOODALL

BORN: April 3, 1934, London, England

MARRIED:
Hugo van Lawick (1964–1974),
Derek Bryceson (1975–1980)

CHILD:
Hugo Eric Louis van Lawick

YOUNG JANE

Valerie Jane Morris-Goodall was born in London, England, in 1934. She began going by Jane as a teen. Jane loved animals from a young age. She gathered worms. She studied chickens in her family's hen house. She even started her own nature club!

Jane's father gave her a toy chimpanzee. Jane has kept the toy all her life.

EARLY INTERESTS

Young Jane loved to read. She often read books about animals in Africa. After graduating from high school, Jane had several jobs. She was a secretary and a waitress. She also worked at a film company.

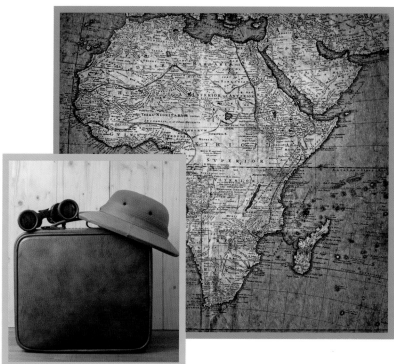

Jane dreamed of traveling to Africa.

Jane began riding horses when she was about 11 years old.

AFRICA

In 1957, Goodall took her first trip to Africa. There she met **archaeologist** Louis Leakey. Leakey made Goodall his assistant. He spoke to her about chimpanzees. There was little **research** on these animals. Goodall decided to study them.

Louis Leakey

Goodall had no research experience, and many people doubted her abilities. But Leakey believed in her.

SETTING UP CAMP

In 1960, Goodall set her plan in motion. She went to Gombe Stream National Park. It is in Tanzania, Africa. Goodall set up camp on a mountainside. She would study a group of nearby chimps in their **habitat**.

Gombe is the smallest park in Tanzania. But more than 100 chimpanzees live there.

LIVING WITH WILD CHIMPS

At first, the chimps avoided Goodall. But she went into the forest each day. She studied the chimps carefully. Goodall also copied their behaviors. Soon, the chimps accepted her. Goodall fed them. She cleaned their fur. She even held the baby chimpanzees.

Goodall gave the chimps lots of bananas.

Goodall still takes careful notes while studying chimps.

INCREDIBLE DISCOVERIES

Chimps use sticks as tools to gather and eat ants.

Goodall learned a lot about chimps. At the time, people thought chimps ate only plants. But Goodall saw them hunt and eat meat. She also saw them make and use tools! This shocked scientists.

FAMILY AND FAME

Hugo van Lawick (left) and Goodall

In 1963, *National Geographic* decided to report on Goodall's work. They sent a **photographer** to Gombe. His name was Hugo van Lawick. He and Goodall got married the next year. Around this time, Goodall wrote an article about Gombe's chimps. She became famous.

Goodall and van Lawick had a son, Hugo.

LEGEND AND TEACHER

In 1977, Goodall founded the Jane Goodall **Institute**. It teaches people about protecting nature. Goodall also started several programs. One is Roots & Shoots. It teaches young people to study nature. Goodall has inspired generations of people to protect chimps and other wildlife.

The Gombe Stream Research Center continues to study wild chimpanzees.

MORE ABOUT GOODALL

Young Jane's nature club was called the ALLIGATOR SOCIETY. Others had to identify animals to join.

Goodall's first chimp encounter was with a male. She named him DAVID GREYBEARD.

Goodall has FACE BLINDNESS. This is a brain disorder. It makes it hard for her to recognize people.

TEST YOUR KNOWLEDGE

1. Where in Tanzania was Goodall's camp?

2. The chimps let Goodall get close to them right away. True or false?

3. What is the name of the youth program Goodall started?

THINK ABOUT IT!

What animal would you want to study? Where does it live?

ANSWERS: 1. Gombe Stream National Park   2. False   3. Roots & Shoots

GLOSSARY

archaeologist – one who studies the remains of people and activities from ancient times.

habitat – the area or environment where a person or animal usually lives.

institute – an organization created for a certain purpose, such as research.

photographer – a person who uses a camera to take pictures.

primate – a mammal with developed hands and feet, a large brain, and a short nose, such as a human, ape, or monkey.

primatologist – one who studies primates.

research – a study of something to learn new information.